I Can Read!

1
READING

CLARK THE SHARK
TOOTH TROUBLE

WRITTEN BY BRUCE HALE   ILLUSTRATED BY GUY FRANCIS

Clark the Shark LOVED reef soccer.

"Flick it and kick it!" he cried.

But sometimes it didn't love him.

POW! "Ouchie-ow-ow!"

Dear Parent:
Your child's love of reading starts here!

Every child learns to read in a different way and at his or her own speed. Some go back and forth between reading levels and read favorite books again and again. Others read through each level in order. You can help your young reader improve and become more confident by encouraging his or her own interests and abilities. From books your child reads with you to the first books he or she reads alone, there are I Can Read Books for every stage of reading:

SHARED READING
Basic language, word repetition, and whimsical illustrations, ideal for sharing with your emergent reader

BEGINNING READING
Short sentences, familiar words, and simple concepts for children eager to read on their own

READING WITH HELP
Engaging stories, longer sentences, and language play for developing readers

READING ALONE
Complex plots, challenging vocabulary, and high-interest topics for the independent reader

ADVANCED READING
Short paragraphs, chapters, and exciting themes for the perfect bridge to chapter books

I Can Read Books have introduced children to the joy of reading since 1957. Featuring award-winning authors and illustrators and a fabulous cast of beloved characters, I Can Read Books set the standard for beginning readers.

A lifetime of discovery begins with the magical words **"I Can Read!"**

Visit www.icanread.com for information
on enriching your child's reading experience.

To the fine folks at Chaucer's Books,
with mucho aloha
—B.H.

To the Francis family dentists,
Dr. Larry, Dr. Lee, and Dr. Bill—
you keep us all smiling
—G.F.

I Can Read Book® is a trademark of HarperCollins Publishers.

Clark the Shark: Tooth Trouble
Copyright © 2015 by HarperCollins Publishers
All rights reserved. Printed in the United States of America.
No part of this book may be used or reproduced in any manner whatsoever without written permission except in the case of brief quotations embodied in critical articles and reviews. For information address HarperCollins Children's Books, a division of HarperCollins Publishers, 195 Broadway, New York, NY 10007.
www.icanread.com

Library of Congress catalog card number: 2013944038
ISBN 978-0-06-227908-8 (trade bdg.) —ISBN 978-0-06-227906-4 (pbk.)

Typography by Sean Boggs

15 16 17 18 PC/WOR 10 9 8 7 6 5 4 3 ❖ First Edition

His tooth hurt.

His tooth wobbled.

What if it fell out of his mouth?

"You need to see a dentist,"
said Miss Mahi, the school nurse.
"What's a dentist?" asked Clark.

"Someone who fixes teeth,"
said Miss Mahi.

"I'll call your mother."

As Clark waited for his mother,

along came his friend Joey Mackerel.

"Check this out," said Clark.

Wiggle wiggle wiggle. "Ow, ow, ow!"

"Cool!" said Joey.

Billy-Ray Ray joined them.

"I'm going to the dentist today,"

said Clark the Shark.

"No way!" said Billy-Ray.

"I hear dentists are scarier

than a box full of blue whales."

"Really?" said Joey.

"REALLY?" said Clark.

"Really and truly," said Billy-Ray.

Uh-oh and oh no!

Clark was worried.

"And dentists are meaner than
a ten-page math test,"
said Billy-Ray Ray.

Uh-oh and oh no!

"Don't listen to him,"

said Joey Mackerel.

"You'll be fine."

Clark wasn't so sure.

When his mother came to get him,

he asked, "Do I HAVE to go?"

"What's wrong?" his mom asked.

"Billy-Ray Ray says dentists
are mean and scary," said Clark.

"Billy-Ray also told you that whales can fly," said his mom.

"Oh, yeah," said Clark.

Then a rhyme popped into his head:

"Don't shed a tear,

'cause there's nothing to fear!"

"That's right," said his mom.

At last, Clark relaxed and smiled.

He was his usual sharky self.

Until . . .

They reached the dentist's office,

and Clark thought a scary thought:

What if Billy-Ray was right?

At the dentist's office, Clark wailed.

He hung on to the door,

and he clung to the chairs.

"No!" he said. "You can't make me!"

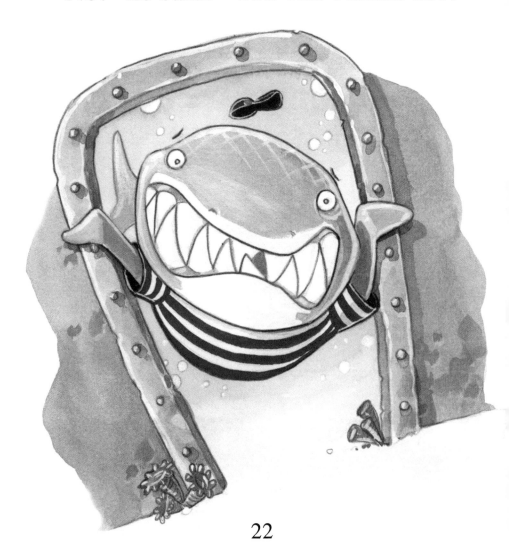

It took his mother, two dads,

and a dental assistant

to get Clark into the dentist's chair.

And then, *uh-oh and oh no . . .*

In came the DENTIST!

"Hi," she said, "I'm Doctor Pia.

What has teeth but cannot eat?"

Clark stared.

Doctor Pia was tiny!

"A comb!" she said. "Get it?"

Doctor Pia juggled her tools.

"What time do you visit a dentist?"

"I don't know," said Clark.

"Tooth-hurty!" she said.

The dentist played happy music.

Doctor Pia was nice!

She had the gentlest fins

and the silliest jokes.

"What's a dentist's favorite animal?" asked Doctor Pia.

"I don't know," said Clark. "What?"

"A molar bear," she said.

They laughed together.

"Ha, ha, HA!" roared Clark.

Doctor Pia worked on his mouth.

And then . . .

"Here's that bad boy," said Dr. Pia.

She held up the tooth.

"The new one will come in soon.

Want a seaweed lollipop?"

The next day, Jocy asked,

"So? Was the dentist scary?"

Clark smiled and said,

"I didn't shed a tear,

'cause there was nothing to fear!"

CLARK THE SHARK'S BITE-SIZED FACTS

1 Sharks have many rows of teeth so they never run out of them. When a shark loses a tooth, another one moves into its place.

2 Sharks lose their teeth more than once— some lose up to 30,000 teeth in their lifetime!

3 Sharks have the most powerful jaws of any animal on the planet.